Let's Make a Lot of Things

The entire text of this book
was written in a calligraphic hand
by Robert W. Galvin

Let's make A LOT OF THINGS

Crafts for Home, School, and Camp

Written and illustrated by

HARRY ZARCHY

ALFRED A. KNOPF ~ NEW YORK

This is a BORZOI BOOK, Published by,
ALFRED A. KNOPF, INC.

To Billy

FOREWORD

Would you like to make a silver ring, or a clay bowl, or a wrought-iron book-end, or a leather wallet? Then this book is for you. It is for people who like to work with their hands and enjoy creating attractive and useful things. Many of the things described in this book can be made at home with a few very simple tools. Even beginners will find the easy-to-follow, step-by-step instructions and drawings practically fool-proof. If you can read, you can be a craftsman. It is as easy as that!

Since good craftsmanship knows no age limits, this book is dedicated to all youngsters who enjoy making things, whether they are six years old, or sixty — but especially to little Billy.

CONTENTS

What to Make

ABOUT METALS

COPPER: Copper is a soft metal that becomes hard and brittle when hammered. When it reaches this state, it must be "annealed." Annealing consists of heating the piece to dull red color, then allowing it to cool. This softens the metal so that it may be worked further. Cold rolled copper is best for craftwork. This may be purchased in sheets. Copper may be hard or soft soldered.

BRASS: Brass is an alloy of copper and zinc. It is harder than copper, and has a somewhat more yellowish color. It, too, must be softened by annealing, and may be made springy by hammering. Brass may be hard or soft soldered.

BRONZE: Bronze, an alloy composed chiefly of copper and tin, is not commonly used in amateur craftwork. Bronze bells are famous for their good tone. A gong may be made by hammering a disk of sheet bronze in even concentric circles. Test the tone by tapping it as the work progresses. Continued hammering will change the tone.

ALUMINUM: Aluminum is suitable for

15

"one piece" craft projects, such as bowls and trays. It cannot be satisfactorily soldered with ordinary equipment. Aluminum pieces are generally joined by riveting. Aluminum can be cut, sawed and filed very easily, and readily accepts texturing. Unlike other metals, which are annealed by heating to a dull red, aluminum is annealed by heating to a pink color in subdued light. It is then permitted to cool slowly.

STERLING SILVER: Sterling silver is an alloy of fine (pure) silver and copper. This makes it more durable, since pure silver is a soft metal, and wears easily. It may be hard or soft soldered. Hammering will harden silver, making annealing necessary. Silver is commonly used for rings, bracelets, and other jewelry that comes in contact with the skin.

NICKEL SILVER: Nickel silver is not silver at all, but is an alloy of copper, zinc and nickel. It is frequently used in craftwork because of its resemblance to silver, and because it does not tarnish easily. It is harder than silver. Nickel silver may be hard or soft soldered, and requires annealing after hammering.

Different metals may be combined to form interesting contrasts of color and texture. For example, a pin may have a copper base, with a nickel silver figure soldered to it. Aluminum may be combined with other metals by riveting. Do not use aluminum for the base of a brooch or pin, since the catch cannot be soldered to it.

About Metal Etching

Certain acids will dissolve, or etch, metals. Nitric acid will etch copper, brass, silver and nickel silver. Some substances are not affected by acids, and are known as acid resists. Black asphaltum varnish is used for craftwork. It is a thick liquid which is thinned with turpentine, for easy brushing.

When an acid resist is painted on a piece of metal as a design, and the metal is then immersed in an acid solution, the acid will eat away all the metal except that which has been painted with the resist. This process is called etching.

Etching may also be accomplished by coating the entire piece with the resist, then scratching out a design on the face, exposing the design on the surface of the metal. When the piece is etched, the

17

design will show up as a series of fine lines. Always permit the asphaltum to dry for twenty-four hours before etching.

PREPARING THE ETCHING BATH: Use a glass, stoneware, crockery or enamelware receptacle for acid. A vessel with a cover is preferable. Pour in the required amount of water first, then add acid slowly. ALWAYS ADD ACID TO WATER. NEVER ADD WATER TO ACID. One part of acid to four parts of water makes a good working solution. Less acid slows the action of the etching bath, more acid speeds it up.

IMPORTANT: Wash acid from hands immediately, useing running water. Wear rubber gloves when handling acid. Wear a rubber apron. Avoid acid on clothing. Do not breathe fumes given off by the etching bath. Work in a well-ventilated spot. Use photographer's tongs to handle work in the acid bath. Label bottle plainly, "ACID-DO NOT TOUCH" and keep it away from little children. Keep acid containers covered when not in use. Used acid solution may be poured back into a clean bottle, using a glass funnel. A tray may be used for etching, then covered with a sheet of glass when it is not in use.

How to Antique Silver

Silver may be antiqued, or darkened, by placing it in a solution of liver of sulphur.

Use a glass, china, or earthenware container for the antiquing bath. Never use copper, brass or any other metal, as this will decompose the chemical quickly.

Mix enough solution to cover the work completely. To one glass of water add a pea-sized lump of liver of sulphur, stirring until it dissolves.

Work to be antiqued is first polished, then washed with a brush, soap, and water. Immerse the work in the solution and agitate it for a few seconds to get rid of air bubbles. When the silver has become sufficiently dark, remove it and allow it to dry. Mild heat will help drying.

Using fine steel wool, rub lightly over the surface of the jewelry. This will remove the antique finish from the high spots, leaving low spots and areas dark.

Solution should be mixed fresh each day, as it will not keep.

Warm water used in making up the antiquing bath will speed the darkening process. This solution may also be used for antiquing copper.

How to Solder

There are two kinds of soldering operations: hard soldering and soft soldering. In hard soldering, silver solder is used. This has a very high melting point, and work to be hard soldered must be brought to red heat. In soft soldering, lead solder is used. This is an alloy which has a low melting point, and work to be soft soldered should not be heated beyond the melting point of the solder.

SOFT SOLDERING

Soft soldering is done on bracelets and other metal work where the soldered joint does not come in contact with the skin, since soft solder contains lead.

Use a blowtorch for soldering jewelry. Blowtorches are fueled with either alcohol or gasoline. An alcohol torch is recommended for all soldering operations called for in this book. The advantage of a blowtorch over a soldering iron is that a perfectly clean joint can be obtained with a torch, whereas a soldering iron always leaves a deposit of solder on the finished surface, which must then be cleaned and scraped.

CLEANING THE JOINT: First, be sure that both surfaces to be joined by soldering are thoroughly clean. Brighten the metal by rubbing with emery cloth, then use a clean rag to wipe the surface. This is important, since solder will not adhere to a dirty surface. Then apply a thin film of soldering flux to both surfaces to be joined.

PREPARING THE SOLDER: Hammer one end of a strip of wire solder on a steel or iron surface until it is about half the thickness of a dime. Then, cut the flattened piece into ⅛" or ¼" squares, using a pair of tin snips or scissors. Use solid wire solder. Acid core solder (hollow wire solder with an acid core), and rosin core solder (hollow wire solder with a rosin core), are both unsuitable for this type of work.

SOLDERING: Place a small piece of cut solder between the two surfaces that you wish to join. Arrange your work on a charcoal block, a sheet of asbestos, a firebrick, or a building brick. You are now ready to apply heat. Allow the flame from a blowtorch to fall directly upon the piece you are soldering. As soon as the work reaches the

21

melting point of the solder, the solder will melt and flow, joining both surfaces. When soldering a small piece to a larger one, the flowing or "running" of the solder may be seen as a bright line appearing around the base of the smaller piece. Remove the torch and allow the soldered work to cool before handling it. Moving work before the solder cools and hardens may result in a weak and faulty joint.

HINTS: It is good practice to bind together pieces that are being soldered. This prevents accidental movement during soldering. Black iron binding wire is best. Work may sometimes be held together with paper clips.

You can solder without a blowtorch: Arrange your work for soldering. Bind all pieces firmly with wire. Grip the work securely in a pair of pliers and hold it over the flame of a gas burner until the solder flows. Remove from the flame and set it down to cool.

All surfaces that are to be soldered must have good contact with each other, otherwise the solder will not flow between them, and an insecure joint will result.

HARD SOLDERING

Hard soldering is done on ring shanks, and on other parts of jewelry where the soldered joint comes in contact with the skin. It is also used where great strength is required of the joint. Silver solder must be used. Since its melting point is very high, (almost as high as that of silver), great heat is required before the solder will flow. An alcohol torch or a gas flame must be used as a source of heat. A soldering iron cannot be used.

PREPARING THE JOINT: As in soft soldering, two things are essential: the joint must be clean, and there must be perfect contact between the two surfaces that are to be soldered together.

PREPARING THE SOLDER: Silver solder comes in either wire or sheet form. The sheet is simply cut into tiny pieces for use, while the wire must first be hammered flat, then cut into pieces.

SOLDERING: Bind all pieces that are to be soldered, firmly, using wire. Then, apply "self-pickling flux" to the joint. While this is still wet, apply a few tiny pieces of solder to the joint. Place the work upon a charcoal block, a sheet of asbestos, a firebrick,

23

or a building brick. Apply heat gently at first to allow the flux to dry, or "boil off." Then, apply full heat. As the work becomes red hot, watch carefully for the solder to melt and flow. This can be seen as a bright line appearing between the pieces that are being soldered. As soon as the solder flows, remove the torch. Allow the piece to cool slowly. Sometimes borax is used as a flux for hard soldering. This calls for added equipment, for the melted borax upon cooling forms "borax glass," a hard, scaly substance that can only be removed properly by heating the work in a copper vessel containing a solution of sulphuric acid. Boiling the work in the acid is called "pickling." "Self-pickling flux" is inexpensive and eliminates the need for pickling, since no borax glass is formed when it is used.

As in soft soldering, small pieces may be hard soldered by first preparing them, and then holding them over a gas flame with a pair of pliers. Remember that the work must reach red heat before the solder will flow. A large pair of pliers or tongs must be used for this purpose.

PROTECTING PREVIOUSLY SOLDERED JOINTS: It is sometimes necessary to solder several pieces together, involving two or three separate soldering operations. Obviously, the heat of the second soldering operation will melt the solder in the first soldered joint. This joint may be protected by covering it with a paste made of yellow ochre (loam) and water. The second joint may then be soldered without fear of injuring or loosening the first joint. The ochre is removed with soap and water, applied with an old toothbrush.

Polishing Metal

All work that is to be polished must first be cleaned well. Scrub the piece with pumice powder, applied with a wet cloth. Examine the work for scratches. Most scratches, unless they are quite deep, may be removed by rubbing with pumice. To remove deep scratches, go over the spot with fine emery cloth, then rub with pumice. Sometimes a carborundum stick, well moistened, is used for removing scratch marks. This must be followed by emery cloth, then by rubbing with pumice.

After the piece has been cleaned with pumice, you are ready for polishing. Tack a strip of soft leather around a flat stick, about 1" wide. Place the tacks in the back of the stick, leaving the face all smooth leather. Prepare two such sticks. One is for Tripoli, the other, for jeweler's rouge.

Rub the Tripoli, (which comes in brick form), on the polishing stick. When the stick has become well charged with abrasive, rub it briskly over the piece to be polished. Apply pressure, for the cutting action of the Tripoli actually removes minute particles of metal. Continue until all pumice marks are removed.

Clean the piece with soap and water, and dry it with a soft cloth. Charge the other stick by rubbing it with jeweler's rouge. Rub this briskly and rapidly over the surface already buffed with Tripoli, until a high gloss is obtained. Apply pressure while buffing.

When working on uneven surfaces that cannot be reached with the flat polishing stick, Tripoli and rouge may be rubbed on a piece of leather or felt, and polishing may be carried on without the stick.

Finished pieces should be washed with soap and water. Use an old toothbrush to get polishing materials out of the deep portions of the work.

If a polishing motor is available, flannel buffing wheels are used for buffing. The buffs are attached to a threaded arbor, or to a tapered spindle. The spindle is preferred to the arbor, because of the ease with which buffing wheels can be changed. When polishing with a motor, start the motor, then charge the buffing wheels by holding either the Tripoli or rouge against them. Work to be polished is held against the lower portion of the wheel, nearest the operator. Use separate buffing wheels for Tripoli and rouge. Finished work should be cleaned and wiped dry, as in hand buffing.

A box of sawdust is handy for drying metalwork. The work to be dried is placed in the sawdust box, and the sawdust scrumbled around it. When removed, the piece will be quite dry.

Transferring Designs to Metal

Designs that are to be cut out of metal must be drawn very accurately on the metal itself. Since a pencil line may not be visible, other methods may be used.

First clean the surface of the metal by scrubbing thoroughly with powdered pumice and water, applied with a cloth. The design may then be transferred with carbon paper. Should the carbon refuse to "take," the metal must be coated with a surface that will accept the carbon impression. This is done by brushing on a thin coat of white tempera paint. Sometimes the paint refuses to brush out smoothly, and instead rolls up into drops. In this event, moisten the brush and rub it on a cake of soap. Then, mix it with a small quantity of paint and apply it to the metal.

After the pencil or carbon image has been applied to the surface of the tempera paint, the design must be applied to the metal itself. Use a sharp pointed instrument to scratch through the paint, into the metal's surface. The tempera paint may then be washed off with water, and the design cut with either a jeweler's saw or tin snips. The instrument used for scratching the metal is called a scriber. The sharp end of an ordinary pencil compass may be used for this purpose.

When marking metal for a painted etching design, another procedure is used. Etching designs are not scratched into the metal, since these scratches would show in the finished product. In this case, clean the surface with pumice and water, then draw directly upon the metal with a pencil. Your pencil lines will serve as guides for painting the design with acid resist. When making an etched line design, the metal is cleaned as before, and then coated all over with acid resist. The design is then scratched through the resist freehand, exposing the metal beneath. The acid eats only the scratched portions of the metal surface, leaving a line design on the piece.

Another method for marking a design that is to be cut out is to simply draw your design on a piece of paper, and then glue it down to the metal with rubber cement. The piece is then cut out with a jeweler's saw, and the paper is peeled off.

ABOUT IRON AND STEEL

Iron is extracted from iron ore in a blast furnace. The furnace is charged with iron ore, coke and flux. The iron ore yields iron; the coke acts as a fuel, and the flux combines with the impurities in the ore to form a mixture known as slag. The iron extracted from a blast furnace is known as pig iron, or cast iron.

CAST IRON: Cast iron is an impure form of iron. Molten cast iron is poured into a sand mold and permitted to harden. This forms a casting. Castings of this metal are very hard and brittle, and are capable of withstanding great compression. They are used to make bases for machinery, drain pipes, stoves and furnaces. Because of its brittle quality, cast iron cannot be bent; neither can it be tempered, forged or welded. It is mainly used in the manufacture of wrought iron and steel. Cast iron is not used as a crafts metal.

WROUGHT IRON: Cast iron is used to manufacture wrought iron. During this process cast iron is melted, then stirred or puddled with a long iron rod. Chemical changes take place in the puddled mass, giving the finished wrought iron a fibrous texture containing thin threads of slag. It is tough and flexible and may be bent or stretched without breaking. It is not hard, like cast iron, but has a high tensile strength. It may be welded, but cannot be tempered.
Because of its toughness and flexibility, wrought iron is an excellent crafts metal. Ornamental gates and fences are made of wrought iron.

STEEL: Steel, like wrought iron, is made from cast

iron. During the manufacture of steel, carbon is added, but other chemical impurities are removed.

Steel for special purposes is made by adding other metals to form an alloy. Nickel, chromium, manganese and tungsten are some metals that are used in combination with steel to produce special alloys for specific purposes. Nickel steel is used for bridges, rails and engine parts; chrome steel is used for bearings, and stamping and crushing machinery; manganese steel is used for burglar-proof safes; tungsten steel is used for high speed cutting tools.

Some steel will bend easily. Generally, the more carbon the steel contains, the less it will bend. Low carbon steel (steel containing a low percentage of carbon) may be used as a substitute for wrought iron.

Steel may be tempered, that is, brought to a specified degree of hardness by means of heat. Page 98 contains directions for making a chasing tool from a piece of tool steel.

ABOUT CLAY

Clay is widely distributed throughout the earth. It is generally thought to be a hydrous silicate of alumina resulting from the decomposition of feldspar and other igneous rocks. It is never found in an absolutely pure state, but is always mixed with some impurities such as sand, iron oxides, crushed rock, lime, magnesia, other minerals and organic matter. These impurities account for the wide range of colors in which natural clays are to be found.

Clays which are sold for craft use have already been washed free of most impurities and mixed with the proper amount of fine sand to prevent the pottery from cracking. However, if you wish to prepare your own clay, here is the proper procedure:

1. Dig the natural clay from a stream bank or other clay deposit.

2. Allow the clay to dry, then break it into very small pieces. This can be done by placing the dried lumps into a sack and pounding with a hammer.

3. Sift the dry clay through a sieve-about ¼" mesh will do. (Make a sieve, using ¼" wire mesh, or hardware cloth.)

4. Fill a pail about half full of water. Sprinkle

the sifted clay into the pail until the clay begins to appear at the top of the water.

5. Allow the mixture to stand for about an hour, then plunge your bare arm into the pail and stir it vigorously.

6. Pour the thick fluid through a sieve made of window screening, into another receptacle. The sieve will hold back small stones but will pemit sand to go through.

7. The resultant mixture is known as "slip." A good supply of slip should be kept on hand at all times. The older slip becomes, the better it will be.

8. After the slip has settled overnight it is necessary to pour off the water that is at the top of the container. This thickens the slip. Pouring off may be necessary several times.

9. For modeling or coil building we must further thicken the slip so that it becomes clay of proper consistency. It should be soft enough so that you can easily indent it with your finger, but not so soft that it will stick to your hands.

10. Pour a quantity of slip on to a plaster tile, or slab. The porous plaster will absorb water from the clay, causing it to become stiff. Remove the clay from the plaster and knead it until it forms

a mass of correct consistency. If it is too hard, sprinkle it with water and continue kneading and wedging. (See p. 37). If it is too soft, slam it against a dry plaster tile several times. This will remove some of the water, thickening the mass. Continue to "condition" the clay until it is ready to be used. If you wish to reclaim hard dry clay from practice pieces that have not been fired, follow steps 2 to 10.

DRYING POTTERY: Too rapid, or uneven drying of a wet piece of pottery will cause it to crack. To avoid this, keep drying pieces out of the sun and wind. Allow pottery to dry in a fairly cool room, if possible. Remove the piece from the plaster base upon which it has been formed as soon as it is hard enough to handle. This may be done by passing a taut wire under the bottom of the piece. If the pottery pieces crack despite drying precautions, a little fine sand added to the clay mixture may help. Use building sand, not beach sand.

KEEPING CLAY MOIST: A large earthenware crock with a well fitting cover makes a fine clay bin in which to keep prepared, conditioned clay. An old wash tub, or a zinc lined box may also be used. Wet pieces may be stored in the clay bin between work periods. If the clay bin is large enough, slip, poured into a larg jar, may also be kept there without fear of its drying out.

If no bin is available, any large, non-porous receptacle may be used in an emergency, provided it is covered with wet cloths.

Pieces may also be prevented from drying between work periods by covering them with wet cloths, the whole then being covered with a piece of oilcloth.

ADDING HANDLES TO POTTERY: Wedge a piece of clay. Roll it out into a rope. Shape the rope to form a handle. Rough up the spots to which the handle will adhere by scratching them with the point of a knife or other sharp instrument. Coat the rough spot with slip, applied with your finger, then press the handle firmly into place, taking care not to move it again. Use your fingers to join the handle to the piece. Smooth the joint with slip so that it appears to be part of the piece. This should be done while the piece is still wet, otherwise the handle will not adhere properly.

"LEATHER HARD" CLAY: If clay is permitted to dry partially, it reaches a state where it becomes "leather hard." In this state it is neither dry nor plastic. It is rather dark in color, but it is still wet. Slip will adhere to it, and it will be possible to ornament the surface by incising designs. If it is permitted to dry past the "leather hard" stage, too much shrinkage takes place, and it becomes difficult to restore it to the state of dampness necessary when working. Keep clay in this condition by covering it with a damp cloth, not wet, or by placing it in the clay bin near an open receptacle filled with water.

About Plaster Tiles

Plaster tiles are used as bases for clay modeling. Before using a tile, soak it in water until it will absorb no more, (when it no longer gives off air bubbles). Remove the tile from the water, allow it to dry for a few minutes, then begin modeling directly upon it. If you attempt to model upon a dry tile, the plaster will absorb water from the clay you are using.

Dry plaster tiles are used to make modeling clay from slip. The slip is poured on the tile, which absorbs water rapidly. When the slip has reached the proper degree of stiffness (due to loss of water which has been absorbed by the tile), it is scraped from the plaster surface, then wedged and kneaded before it is used for pottery or modeling.

Tiles which have become saturated with water may be dried rapidly by placing them in the sun, or they may dry slowly indoors. They may be used over and over again.

Wedging Clay

Before firing a piece of clay, be certain that it contains no air bubbles, otherwise the rapid expansion of the air trapped in the clay would cause the side of the piece being fired to blow out. Wedging is a process of kneading and pounding clay to remove all air bubbles and bring the clay to proper working consistency.

HOW TO WEDGE CLAY: Pick up a handful of clay. Slam it down on the wedging board. Repeat the picking up and slamming down of the clay several times. Then, holding the clay in both hands, cut it in half by bringing it down over the taut wire on the wedging board. Examine the cut halves for air bubbles. If there are any present, continue to cut the clay into halves, slamming the halves together on the board. When the cut portions show an even, smooth texture, the clay is in proper working condition.

The wedging board is also used when other materials, such as grog, or sand, must be added to clay.

ABOUT LEATHER

Leather has been used by man for thousands and thousands of years. The early cavemen probably used leather. Egyptian hieroglyphic writings tell us that leather articles were used as temple offerings as far back as five thousand years ago. The ancient Hebrews were the first people to make use of oak bark as a tanning agent. Basically the same process is used today in the preparation of much of our present day leather.

Leather has been used for a great variety of purposes. The Romans used leather for armor.

38

It has been used for drinking vessels, clothing, shoes, wigwams, bookbindings, animal harnesses, and many other things. The deerskin of the American Indian has never been surpassed for its softness and its ability to resist water.
There are two types of leather: chrome tanned, and vegetable, or bark tanned. Only bark tanned leathers are suitable for tooling and it is among these that we find our leathers for crafts purposes.

CALFSKIN is the most commonly used craft leather. It takes tooling beautifully, and the heavier grades may be carved. It comes in a variety of colors, and has a soft, rich finish.

TOOLING COWHIDE is excellent for projects involving heavier leather, such as knife or axe sheaths, camera cases, and the like. Heavy cowhide may be carved.

OOZE COWHIDE is a heavy leather with a velvet finish. It can be tooled or carved.

MOROCCO is a goatskin with a beautiful grain. It is widely used for craft work, and is suitable for billfolds, purses, bookcovers, bookbindings,

and other articles which must resist wear.
Cheaper leathers are frequently embossed to imi-
tate Morocco. It is available in various dark, rich
colors.

TOOLING SHEEPSKIN is sometimes used as a substitute for calfskin, where expense is a factor. It
tools easily, but is neither as strong nor as good-
looking as calfskin. The leather is very delicate,
and shows marks readily.

PIGSKIN may be tooled with simple line designs.
It is strong, has an unusual texture, and resists
wear—in fact, its appearance improves with age.

SNAKE, ALLIGATOR, LIZARD, and OSTRICH skins
are beautiful leathers suitable for unusual, ex-
pensive jobs. They are not toolable, and are not
always available at supply houses. Their high
price prohibits their general use. Other leathers
are embossed to resemble them.
Leather may be purchased by the hide (from a
large animal), the skin (from a small animal), by
the side (half a hide), by the half skin, by the
square foot, and in special sizes cut to order.
Some crafts supply houses offer kits containing

ready cut parts for assembling into finished articles. It is also possible to purchase scrap leather by the pound. These pieces of assorted leathers may be used for small projects

Leather Lacing

Use 3/32″ lacing for all projects described in this book. This lacing is made of goatskin, and comes in a variety of colors. A #0 punch or thonging chisel is used for this size lacing.

When lacing a piece of craftwork, pull the lace up just tight enough to make a snug fit against the edge of the work. Do not pull too tight, otherwise the edge of the piece, particularly if the leather is soft, may be distorted.

When using the thonging chisel, the work to be punched is placed on a maple board. A line is marked about 1/8″ from the edge, and the slits are punched on this line. This results in a somewhat neater job than punching round holes, but requires more care in handling. Before the lace is passed through, each hole must be enlarged just enough to admit the pointed end of the lace. A fid is used for this purpose.

JEWELRY & METALWORK TOOLS

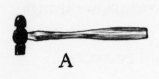

BALL PEEN HAMMER: for driving chisels, punches and other metal tools. Round end used for spreading rivet heads and for texturing metals, (fig. A).

A

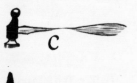

PLANISHING HAMMER: used to produce the bright, faceted marks seen on some metalwork, (fig. B).

B

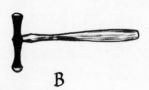

CHASING HAMMER: used with chasing tools, generally useful, (fig. C).

C

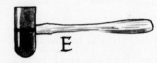

RIVETING HAMMER: flat face used for hammering down rivets, thin end for texturing metalwork, (fig. D).

D

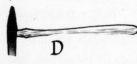

MALLET: for straightening and flattening metal without leaving marks. Available in many shapes and sizes, (fig. E).

E

F ALCOHOL TORCH (Mouth): For small pointed flame, light the wick, blow through rubber tube, (fig. F).

G ALCOHOL TORCH (Automatic): delivers a steady flame suitable for hard soldering, (fig. G).

H TIN SNIPS: used for cutting sheet metal, (fig. H).

I HAND DRILL: Twist drills up to ¼" are inserted in the chuck (arrow), (fig. I).

J TWIST DRILL: used in hand drill for either metal or wood, (fig. J).

K FLUTED DRILL POINT: used in hand drill for wood, or very soft metals only, (fig. K).

JEWELRY & METALWORK TOOLS

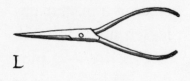

L

CHAIN NOSE PLIERS: for shaping wire and small pieces, (fig. L).

M

COMBINATION PLIERS (Slip-joint pliers): for work requiring large gripping tool, (fig. M).

N

END CUTTING NIPPERS: for fine jewelry work, cutting wire, small rivets, etc, (fig. N).

O

LINEMAN'S PLIERS: for cutting heavier wire and electric wiring, (fig. O).

P

TWEEZERS: for handling small pieces of jewelry, findings, and gem stones, (fig. P).

Q

FILES: Every shop needs flat, triangular and half-round files, (fig. Q).

R

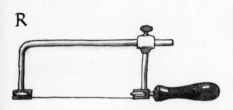

JEWELER'S SAW: Changing blades is a matter of loosening two thumb screws. No's. #3/o and #4/o blades should be used for all fine sheet metal sawing, (fig. R).

S

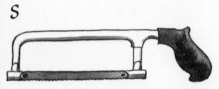

HACK SAW: for cutting metal rods, tubes, bars, wrought iron. Use blade having 18 or 24 teeth to the inch, (fig. S).

T

CENTER PUNCH: driven lightly with hammer to make mark in metal that is to be drilled, (fig. T).

U

DAPPING DIE: a steel block used to produce domes in sheet metal, (fig. U).

V

DAPPING PUNCH: comes in various sizes, to match holes in dapping die, (fig. V).

JEWELRY & METALWORK TOOLS
CONTINUED

X

SCRIBER: for marking sheet metal for cutting, (fig. X).

RING MANDREL: a tapered steel bar, marked off into ring sizes, used for forming rings and other small bands, (fig. Y).

Y

Z

RING GAUGE: used only for gauging ring sizes, not hard enough for forming operations, (fig. Z).

a

RING SIZES: Each ring is stamped with a size. Select the one that fits, then form the band to fit the size on the ring mandrel, (fig. a).

RING CLAMP: Rings are inserted between jaws. Wedge is tapped between opposite jaws to hold work firmly, (fig. b).

b

MACHINIST'S VISE: for holding pieces for almost all metalworking operations. Larger sizes hold wrought iron for riveting, drilling, bending, (fig. c).

c

JEWELRY FINDINGS

A

B

JEWELRY FINDINGS: Catches, (fig. A) and joints, (fig. B) are used in pairs on the backs of pins and brooches. After the catch and joint are soft-soldered to the back, the pintong is fitted into place. Sometimes it is held in place with a small wire rivet, and at other times it is merely pressed into place with pliers.

C

PIN BACK UNIT: An entire assembly, consisting of a bar, to which is fastened a pin-joint-catch unit, may be soft-soldered to metal brooches. These units are also cemented to the backs of plastic pins, and may be used to make unusual brooches from large, decorative buttons, (fig. C).

D

EAR WIRE: This is soldered to the back of a completed ear ring. Soft solder is used, (fig. D).

How to Use the JEWELER'S SAW

A

Make a bench fork by cutting a notch in the end of a 4"x 8" board, (fig. A).

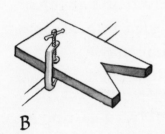

B

Use "C" clamp to fasten bench fork to the projecting edge of a desk or table. The notched end should project over the edge, (fig. B).

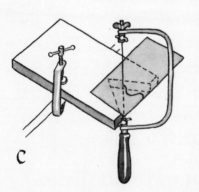

C

Hold saw vertically, with handle below the work to be cut. Rest the blade against the metal and saw up and down firmly, but with little or no pressure applied. The weight of the blade against the work will provide good cutting action, (fig. C).

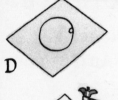

D

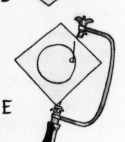

E

HOW TO CUT
INSIDE CIRCLES:

Mark circle to be cut on metal. Drill a ⅛" hole just inside circle, (fig. D). (See p. 27). Loosen one end of saw blade, pass it through the drilled hole, then re-clamp it in frame, (fig. E). Use bench fork, keeping saw upright at all times. To cut around a curve, keep sawing up and down, curving the saw gently.

A machinist's vise is useful for sawing small work, (figF).

F

HINTS:

Blade teeth always point down. To loosen blade, twist handle and thumb screw at top of frame, (fig. G). Thumb screws (→) hold blade in place. Keep blade taut when sawing. To saw abrupt curves, keep moving saw up and down in the same position to provide clearance for the turn.

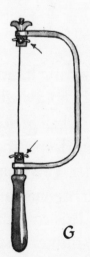

G

TEXTURING METAL SURFACES

Work to be textured must rest upon a smooth block of iron or steel. An old flatiron makes a good working surface.

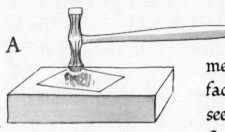

A

PLANISHING
Planishing hammers make the bright, faceted marks sometimes seen on metal craftwork. Overlapping hammer marks (round, oval, or square, depending upon the shape of the hammer) are applied while the piece is flat. Bowls and trays are then raised into shape, (fig. A).

B

PEENING
In the absence of a planishing hammer, an effect similar to planishing may be obtained by striking the metal with the round end of a ball peen hammer, (fig. B). The resulting marks will be deeper than planishing marks, and somewhat smaller. This hammer leaves a round mark.

"Spotting" may also be done with the ball peen hammer. This consists of making scattered marks with the hammer instead of covering an area solidly.

RIVETING HAMMER

A riveting hammer may be used to texture metal. This type of marking is limited in its application, since the riveting hammer leaves a straight, narrow mark. This may be applied to border areas such as picture frames, and the rims of bowls and trays, (fig. C).

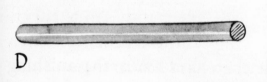

C

CHASING TOOLS

Chasing tools are made of short lengths of steel rod. They act as stamps, leaving an impression in softer metals into which they are driven. The tool is held vertically against the work, then struck smartly with a hammer. A chased background causes a design to stand out, (fig. E).

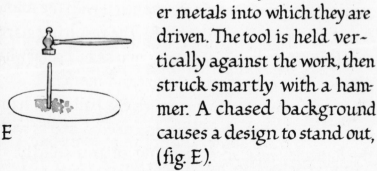

D

E

KNOT RING

MATERIALS: Sterling silver wire, 16 or 18 gauge, silver solder, self-pickling flux, charcoal block, alcohol torch, file, pliers, vise

A

Cut two 3" pieces of silver wire. Bend one piece to form a knot in the center, as in fig. A.

B

Bend the second piece of wire to form an inter~ locking knot as in fig. B.

Tighten the knot by placing one end of each wire in a vise, then pulling with a pair of pliers, (fig C). Bind together the two wires which form the shank, then hard solder them. This will make it easier to shape the ring.

C

D

Use a mallet to hammer the ring to shape, either on a ring mandrel, or on a hardwood dowel.

File the ends square as in fig. D, then hard solder the joint to complete the ring. (For polishing directions, see p. 25).

(For polishing directions, see p. 25).

WIRE BAND DESIGNS

A

A simple band is made by placing the ends of two lengths of wire in a vise and twisting the other ends, (fig. A).

B

Solder three parallel strips of wire together to form a simple band, (fig. B).

Cut pieces of wire into exact lengths. Place the pieces upon a charcoal block, brick, or asbestos surface. Apply blowtorch heat. Each wire length will melt and roll up into a little ball, called shot. Solder them between two pieces of straight wire, (fig. C). (See p. 74 for chain soldering directions).

D

Clamp the ends of three pieces of wire in a vise. Use pliers to braid them. Solder the braided strip, then hammer flat, (fig. D).

SNAKE RING

MATERIALS: scrap wire, silver wire, 16 gauge or heavier, file, wire cutters, sol~ dering equipment (alcohol torch, self~pickling flux, silver solder)

A

Wrap a 10" length of scrap wire around a twig, dowel or tube that is exactly the same thickness as the finger upon which the ring is to be worn. Cut the wire so that both ends are visible from the top, (fig. A).

Unwind the coiled scrap wire and use it to measure a similar length of silver wire, 16 gauge or heavier. If the scrap wire is thin~ ner than the silver wire, cut the silver wire about ½" longer.

B

Hammer one end of the wire to flatten it slightly, then file it to resemble a snake's head. Taper the other end with a file, then file notches in the tapered portion to re~ semble rattles, (fig. B).

C

Wrap the snake around the form previou͡ly used, then re-move it, and solder the coils together, as in fig. C. (See p. 23 for soldering instructions).

The ring is now very soft, and in order to harden it, it must be hammered upon a hard surface. Use a ring mandrel, or if that is not available, a length of ¼" or 3/8"

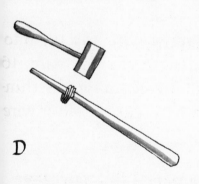

D

pipe held firmly in a vise. The ring need not fit the pipe. Hammer with a mallet, rota~ting the ring and striking in the same place, (fig. D).

Scrub the ring with an old tooth brush dipped in powdered pumice or kitchen cleanser. Buff the ring to a polish. (See p. 25).

SHEET SILVER RING

MATERIALS: 18 gauge sterling silver or nickel silver, ring mandrel, jeweler's saw, torch, hard solder, self-pickling flux, charcoal block, fine emery cloth.

A

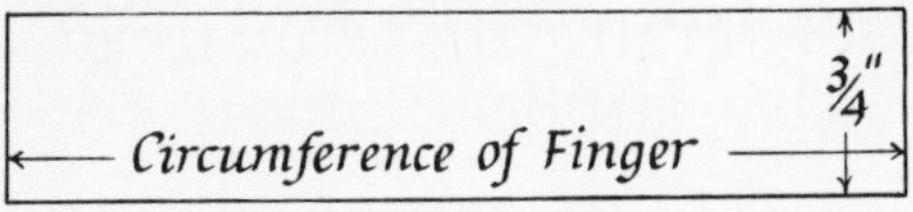

Cut a piece of paper ¾" wide and as long as the circumference of the finger upon which it is to be worn, (fig. A).

B

Fold the paper in half lengthwise as in fig. B

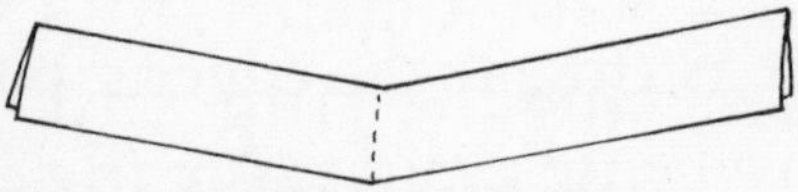

C

Now fold it in half as in fig. C.

D

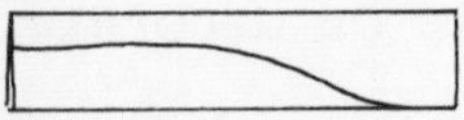

E

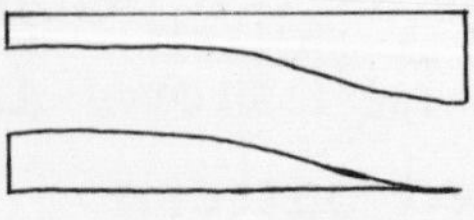

Mark a pencil line (fig D) on the folded strip. The thin portion represents the shank of the ring, the wide portion, the top.

Cut away the bottom portion of the pattern, (fig E).

56

F

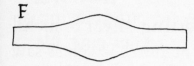

The paper pattern when opened should look like fig. F.

A little practice will enable you to control the width of the shank and top.

G

Use rubber cement to paste the paper pattern to the sheet metal (silver or nickel silver). First, coat the paper lightly, then coat the metal. After a few minutes, press the paper upon the metal. Do not paste the pattern to the center of the sheet, but keep it as close to the edge as possible in order to avoid waste, (fig. G).

H

Use a jeweler's saw to cut out ring form, (fig. H). (See p. 48).

If the top of the ring is to be decorated

I

J

with a pierced design, it should be cut before the paper pattern is unfolded. Fig. I shows a small figure cut from the folded pattern. Fig. J shows the pattern unfolded.

SHEET SILVER RING

Use jeweler's saw to cut out your initial. Hard solder initial to top of ring blank as in fig. K. (See p. 23).

K

L

Shape the ring by hammering it around a ring mandrel, or as follows: prepare a lead block by melting scrap lead and pouring it into a jar cover. With a ball peen hammer, shape a groove in the block, (fig. L).

A form for shaping rings may also be made by carving a groove in the end grain of a block of hardwood. A gouge is used for this purpose, (fig. M).

M

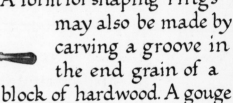

N

Lay the ring blank over the groove, and over it place a hardwood dowel, or a metal rod. Hammering on the dowel will shape the ring, (fig. N).

O

Place ring, face down, upon a charcoal block or sheet of as - bestos, (fig. O). Be sure the ends are filed so that they fit perfectly. Charge the joint with flux and hard solder. Solder the joint.

Use a fine file, then emery cloth, to shape the ring in its final form. The shank may be filed half-round, (fig. P).

P

Clean the ring by rubbing it with a wet cloth that has been dipped in pumice powder. If de - sired, antique it, then polish. (See pp. 19, 25).

STERLING SILVER RING

MATERIALS: jeweler's saw or tin snips, flat file, fine cut, round nose pliers, mallet, solder, flux, blow torch, charcoal block, sterling silver, 16 gauge

A

Use jeweler's saw or tin snips to cut silver into ¾" square, (fig. A).

B

Hammer flat, using mallet.

File edges flat, round corners slightly, (fig. B).

C

Cut another square, smaller than the first. Flatten and file as before. Solder to larger square as in fig. C.

D

Cut a paper strip ⅛" wide, long enough to wrap around finger, (fig. D).

E   F

Cut metal strip same size, bend with round nose pliers as in fig. E.

G

File ends flat, (fig. F). Shank stands over top piece as in fig. G. Apply flux and solder, then heat to weld the joint, (See p. 23).

H

Finished ring appears at fig. H. (See p. 25 for polishing instructions).

SUGGESTED DESIGNS FOR FLAT RINGS

SHEET METAL RING PATTERNS

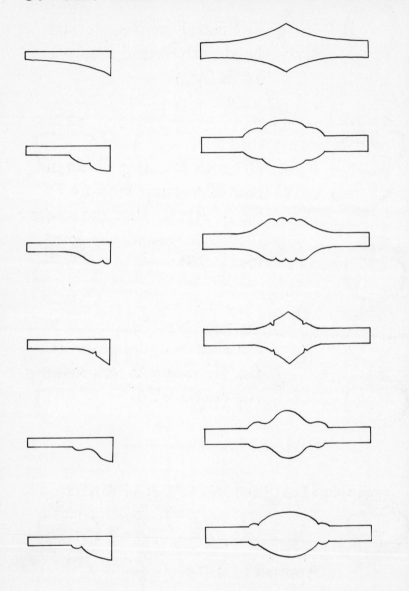

SHEET METAL RING IDEAS

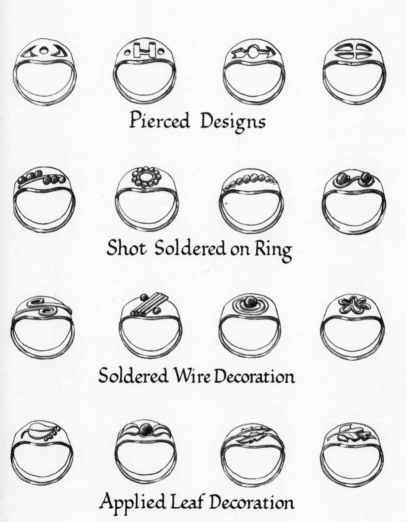

Pierced Designs

Shot Soldered on Ring

Soldered Wire Decoration

Applied Leaf Decoration

BROOCH DESIGNS
For Sheet Metal

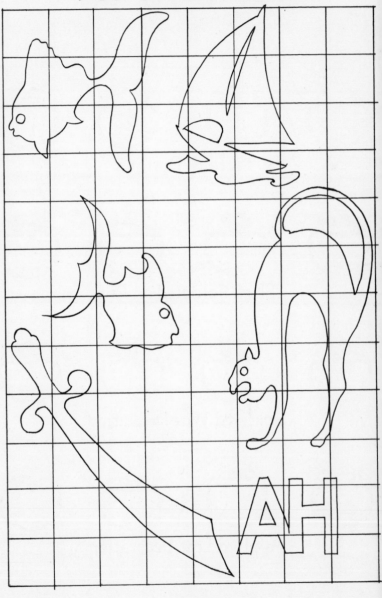

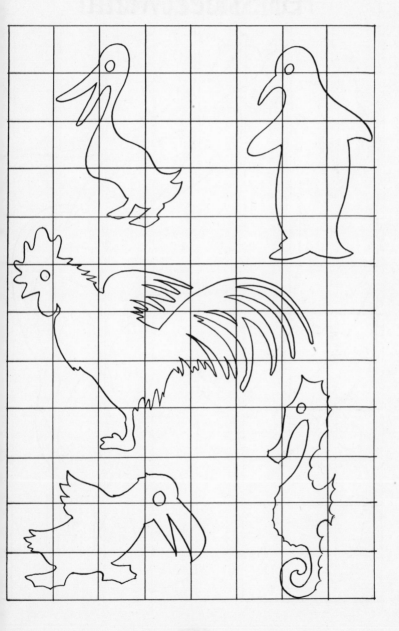

BROOCH DESIGNS
For Sheet Metal

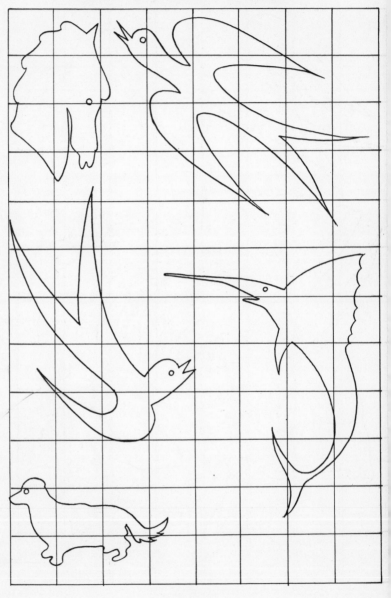

SETTING STONES into Craft Jewelry

Only cabochon stones (stones with a flat base and a round, or domed top) can be set by this method.

Some stones used are carnelian, lapis lazuli, agate, turquoise, jasper, quartz and garnet.

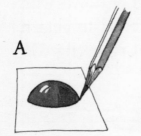

A

TO MAKE A BEZEL:
Trace the outline of the stone, (fig. A).

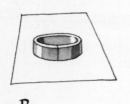

B

Cut a strip of 28 gauge silver, ¼" wide. Anneal it, then bend around pencil line. File ends to perfect fit, then solder to form a ring, (fig. B).

C

Using silver wire (about 20 gauge), form a ring, or bearing to fit snug inside rim, (fig. C).

Solder bearing inside the rim, about ⅛" below the top, (fig. D).

D

The stone will rest upon the bearing as in cross-section, (fig. E).

E

Cover ring mandrel or dowel with emery cloth. Rub bezel to obtain curve, (fig. F), to fit ring, (fig. G).

F

H

Bezels for flat pins need no curved bottoms, (fig. H).

G

SETTING STONES: File upper edge of bezel inward, (fig. I). With stone in place, force bezel against stone with a burnisher, (fig. J).

I   J

SIMPLE EARRINGS

MATERIALS: sterling silver, nickel silver or copper, tin snips or jeweler's saw, wood mallet, solder, soldering flux, asbestos sheet, charcoal block or brick, ear screws, file

Use tin snips to cut two 3/4" squares of metal, or saw metal to size with jeweler's saw. (See p. 48 for instructions).

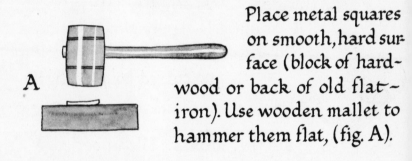

Place metal squares on smooth, hard surface (block of hard-wood or back of old flat-iron). Use wooden mallet to hammer them flat, (fig. A).

A

File all edges straight, then file corners slighly round, (fig. B).

B

Prepare one side of each metal piece for soldering. (See p. 20 for soldering instructions). Soft solder may be used. Brighten sides that are to be joined, using steel wool. Apply a very thin coat of soldering flux. Hammer a piece of soft solder to paper thickness, then cut about ¼" square and place between metal squares, (fig. C).

Arrange squares slightly overlapping, as in fig. D. Apply blowtorch heat. When solder flows, permit piece to cool.

Solder ear screws into place: Brighten both surfaces to be joined, apply thin layer of flux, deposit small bit of solder at the joint, then apply heat until solder flows, (fig. E).

In fig. F ear screw is soldered near upper edge of piece, causing earring to hang low. In fig. G screw is soldered near center causing earring to cover lobe of ear.

71

SOLDERED BRACELET

MATERIALS : copper, or nickel silver, 1½″ x 6″
jeweler's saw or tin snips, emery cloth,
file, mallet, steel wool, solder, flux,
blowtorch, soldering block

A

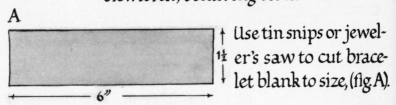

↑
1½
↓

Use tin snips or jewel-
er's saw to cut brace-
let blank to size, (fig. A).

← 6″ →

↑
1½″
↓

Use tin snips or jewel-
er's saw to cut wedge
shapes, (fig. B). File

B

edges of blank and wedge shapes,
then smooth with emery cloth.

Hammer all pieces flat
Use wooden mallet, ham-
mering metal on hard-
wood block or smooth
metal surface, (fig. C).

C

Brighten all pieces with steel wool.

D

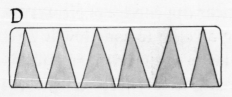

Arrange wedge pieces
on blank in position
for soldering, (fig. D).

SOLDERING THE BRACELET: Coat the under surface of each wedge with a thin film of flux. Replace it in the same position, first placing a piece of thin hammered solder, about ⅛" square, directly under it.

Use a blowtorch, applying heat gradually and evenly over the piece. Do not overheat. Molten solder will be seen as a bright line around each wedge. Cool bracelet slowly. Re-solder loose wedges, cleaning joints first. If too much solder has been used, scrape off excess with penknife and then use steel wool.

E

Bend bracelet to shape by hammering around a baseball bat, using mallet.(figE)

Scour piece with steel wool, then polish. (See p. 25). Entire bracelet may be antiqued by immersing in solution of potassium sulphide and water. Dissolve a pea-sized lump in half glass of warm water. For darker tones, use more potassium sulphide, also known as liver of sulphur. Allow piece to dry, then polish the highlights.

HOW TO MAKE CHAIN

Use silver wire. Simple chain is made by bending loops which interlock. The ends are filed to fit snugly together, (fig. A). Solder each link for strength.

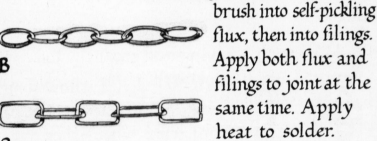

A

TO SOLDER CHAIN: Prepare filings from *Easy Flow Hard Solder.* Dip brush into self-pickling flux, then into filings. Apply both flux and filings to joint at the same time. Apply heat to solder.

B

C

To make identical links, wrap wire around a nail or rod, making a close coil. Slip coil off nail and cut each turn off with a jeweler's saw, creating round links.

D

E

F

FIGURES B, C, D, E, F SHOW CHAIN IDEAS

To make fancy chain, first make each link, (fig. G).

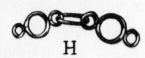

Assemble chain by using binder links, (fig. H).

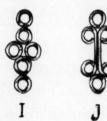

Figures I, J, K, L show some link designs. They may be connected with either one binder link, as in fig. H, or with three links, as in fig. F.

Use chain nose pliers for this work.

75

FOREIGN COIN BRACELET

Coins are held together with links. (See p.74 for link and chain making).

Simplest method is to drill one hole in each side of coin, and then to link coins as in fig. A. Coins held with single links have a tendency to turn on the wrist.

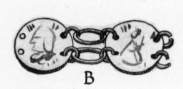

A

Double links are recommended for bracelets, as in fig. B.

B

Fig. C shows variation of double link idea. The only difference is that a single link connects the two coins, instead of two oval links as in fig. B.

C

To fasten ends of bracelets together, prepare one end with a wide link as in fig. D and another end with a "T" shaped wire, as in fig. E. The two are held together by passing the "T" shaped end through the large link, (fig. F).

D   E   F

76

Coins may also be doubled, to form wider bracelets, (fig G).

G

Necklaces may be formed by grad-uating the sizes of the coins used, (fig. H).

H

To drill holes in coins: Mark the spot to be drilled with a center punch, (fig. I). Place the coin in a vise, then use a small drill to make the link holes, (fig. J).

I

J

Links may be either soft or hard soldered after they are closed. Do not attempt to solder on a tar-nished area, but first clean the spot with steel wool.

ETCHED BRACELET~*Line Etch*

MATERIALS: sheet copper or nickel silver, 16 or 18 gauge, metal snips, file, emery cloth, black asphaltum varnish, nitric acid, sharp pointed instrument for scratching design

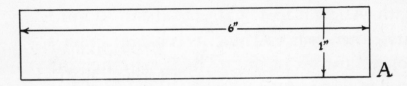

A

Use tin snips to cut sheet metal as in fig. A. Corners may be slightly rounded. Smooth entire piece with emery cloth.

Brush black asphaltum varnish over one entire face, and all edges of the bracelet blank. Dry for 24 hours, then paint rest of

B

blank so that both sides and all edges are completely covered with asphaltum. Dry over night.

Using phonograph needle or similar tool, scratch design into one side of the bracelet, through the asphaltum coating, exposing the surface of the metal, (fig. B).

Slide the bracelet, design up, into the acid bath. Allow it to remain for about 20 minutes, then remove it, using photographer's tongs, and examine it to see whether the etched line is deep enough. If etching is incomplete, return the metal to the acid. When etching is complete, remove the piece and wash it in running water to remove all traces of acid. Use the tongs for this purpose.

Rub the entire piece with a cloth saturated with turpentine. This will remove the asphaltum. Remove traces of asphaltum by scouring with pumice powder.

Bracelet may be polished further, if desired. (See p. 25).

ETCHED BRACELET~*Broad Etch*

MATERIALS: black asphaltum varnish, small pointed brush, nitric acid, wood mallet, sheet copper or nickel silver, 16 or 18 gauge, fine pumice powder, file, emery paper or cloth, carbon paper, tin snips

Use tin snips to cut sheet metal to size, (fig. A).

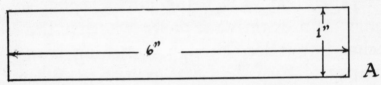

6" 1" A

Pound metal flat with a mallet.

File all corners slightly round. Smooth surfaces and all edges with emery cloth. Next, scrub metal with a wet cloth pad dipped in pumice powder until it is clean and bright. Dry well with clean cloth.

Place blank on scrap of wood and brush black asphaltum varnish over one entire face and all edges, so that no metal shows anywhere. This is to be the back of the bracelet. Dry over night.

B

Now place bracelet blank unpainted side up. This is the face upon which we shall etch our design. Use pencil to draw your design on the clean metal face. Do not scribe the design on the surface, (fig. B).

C

Paint the design with a small pointed brush, using asphaltum varnish. Dry over night, (fig. C).

Prepare the etching bath, and etch the bracelet, following directions on p. 17.

All exposed metal in the design will be eaten away, leaving the painted portions, which resist the acid, raised.

Remove the asphaltum by rubbing with a cloth that has been saturated with turpentine.

Bend bracelet to shape by hammering around a baseball bat, then polish it as desired, (See p. 25)

Interesting effects can be obtained by painting free-hand designs on bracelet before etching. See p. 82 for suggested broad etch designs.

BRACELET DESIGNS-*Broad Etch*

BRACELET DESIGNS- *Line Etch*

Jane Smith
1974 Bayview Road
Fairville, Conn.

WITH LOVE TO MOTHER

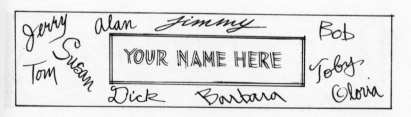

Jerry Alan Jimmy Bob
YOUR NAME HERE
Tom Susan Toby.
Dick Barbara Gloria

PIERCED BRACELET

MATERIALS: strip of bracelet stock, 2"x 6" (copper, aluminum, nickel silver, brass), bench fork, jeweler's saw frame and blades, hand drill and 1/16" drill, file, emery cloth or paper, scriber, rubber cement.

Use tin snips to cut bracelet blank, 2"x 6". File corners slightly round, (fig. A). Clean metal with emery cloth.

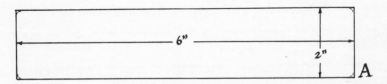

A

Draw design on paper and fasten to metal, (fig B).

B

Drill holes where indicated in fig. C in order to cut inside shapes with saw. Use drill of proper size for circular parts.

C

84

PIERCED BRACELET

Loosen top of jeweler's saw blade. Pass blade through hole in the portion of the design to be cut. Now fasten blade in the saw frame, making blade taut. Place work over bench fork and cut inside pencil lines on the paper. Repeat process for every part of the design that is to be cut out.

When piercing has been completed, remove the paper and polish the surface of bracelet with emery cloth. Inside shapes may be filed, using needle files. If no needle files are available, roll a small strip of emery cloth into a cylinder and use it as a file. (See p.25 for polishing directions).

IDEAS FOR OTHER PIERCED BRACELETS

85

RIVETED BRACELET

MATERIALS:
16 or 18 gauge nickel silver, 2"x 6"
16 or 18 gauge copper, ½" x 6"
5 rivets (copper, brass or aluminum)
to fit 1/16" hole, 1/16" twist drill, hand
drill, ball peen or riveting hammer,
"C" clamp, file, #00 emery cloth,
steel block or anvil, tin snips,
center punch

Cut strip of nickel silver 2"x 6". Cut
strip of copper ½" x 6". Use tin snips.
File all edges, then smooth with
emery cloth.

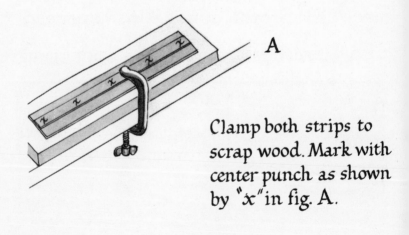

A

Clamp both strips to
scrap wood. Mark with
center punch as shown
by "x" in fig. A.

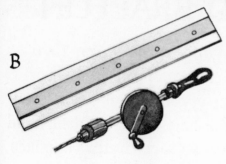

B

Drill a 1/16" hole through both pieces at each mark. Pass a rivet through each hole, and rivet both pieces together, (fig. B).

HOW TO RIVET (FIG. C).

1. Rivet in place.

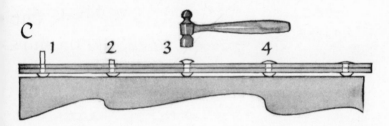

C

2. Cut off with cutting pliers, leaving 1/16".

3. and 4. Mushroom rivet down, forming a shallow, domed head.

D

Shape bracelet by hammering around a baseball bat, (fig. D).

BENDING WROUGHT IRON

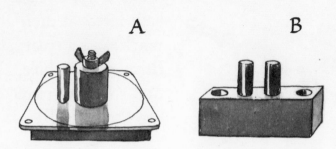

A   B

Adjustable bending jig is either clamped in a vise or screwed to a table. Thumb screw loosens to permit varying width between posts, (fig. A).

Fig. B shows simple jig which is clamped in vise. Width between posts is adjustable by inserting posts into different holes.

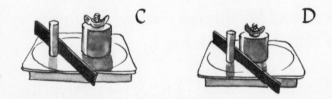

C   D

Fig. C shows posts too far apart. Fig. D shows correct width.

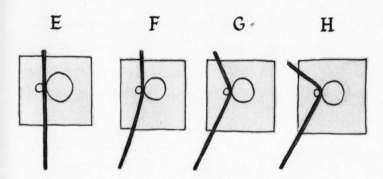

Figs. E, F, G, H show how the jig is used to bend angles.

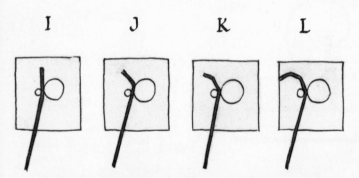

Curves are formed by actually bending shallow angles, close together, (figures I, J, K, L).

PIN-UP LAMP

MATERIALS : cold rolled iron, ⅟₁₆" x ¾", 1 piece 32"
long, 1 piece 12" long, 1 piece 9" long,
hand drill and ⅛" drill, iron rivets to
fit ⅛" hole, center punch, metal
bending jig, 1 ⅜" x 1" nipple,
2 ⅜" hex nuts, 1 key socket,
1 male plug, 6 ft. lampcord

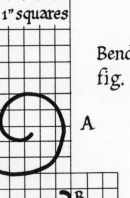

1" squares

Bend 32" piece of iron as in
fig. A. (See p. 88).

Bend 9" piece of iron as
in fig. B.

Bend 12" piece of iron
as in fig. C.

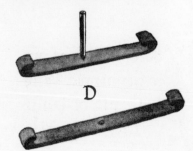

Mark with center punch,
then drill ⅛" hole in center of each piece, (fig. D).

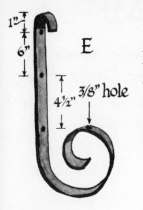

Drill ⅛" holes, as in fig. E. For ⅜" hole, first drill with ¼", then enlarge with ⅜" drill held in bit brace.

Rivet cross pieces in place, as in fig. F.

Insert ⅜" x 1" nipple in ⅜" hole, fig. G.

Fasten nipple in place by tightening two ⅜" hex nuts in place as in fig. H.

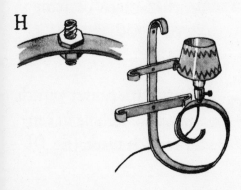

Screw a socket on to the nipple. Wire with 6 ft. of lamp-cord. (See p. 92).

WIRING SOCKETS & PLUGS

MATERIALS : key socket, lamp cord, screw driver, sharp knife

WIRING A SOCKET

Press at point marked "x" in fig. A. Pry off socket cap with a screw driver.

Push one end of the lamp cord through the cap. With sharp knife, cut away 3" of the cotton covering, leaving two insulated wires. Do not cut into the wires, (fig. B).

Make an Underwriter's Knot. (See opposite page). Remove socket unit from shell. Bare enough wire to permit winding once around the connecting screws, clockwise, (fig. C). Tighten the screws.

Replace the socket in the shell, and snap the cap back into place.

WIRING A MALE PLUG

Push one end of the lamp cord through the plug, (fig. D).
Make an Underwriter's Knot. (See instructions at bottom of this page).
Pull the lamp cord down, so that the knot is firm against the bottom of the plug.

D

Bring each lead around a prong, (fig. E).

Bare just enough wire to go around each screw, clockwise. Tighten screws.

E

HOW TO MAKE AN UNDERWRITER'S KNOT:

Wrought Iron HOUSE MARKER

MATERIALS: wood, 3/4" x 7⅝" x 15"

2 pcs. cold-rolled iron, ⅛" x ½" x 12"

1 pc. cold-rolled iron, ⅛" x ½" x 24"

1 pc. cold-rolled iron, ⅛" x ½" x 18"

hack saw, ⅛" drill, ⅛" iron rivets, sandpaper, spar varnish

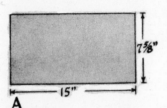

A — 7⅝" — 15"

Cut wood as in fig. A.

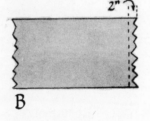

B — 2"

Cut edges as in fig. B.

Sandpaper wood smooth, apply walnut or mahogany stain, when dry, apply spar varnish.

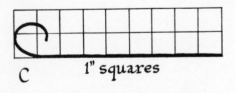

C — 1" squares

Bend both 12" iron pieces as in fig. C. (See p. 88 for bending instructions).

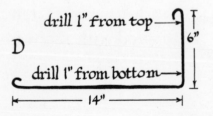

D — drill 1" from top — 6" — drill 1" from bottom — 14"

Bend the 24" piece of iron as in fig. D. Drill ⅛" holes where indicated.

94

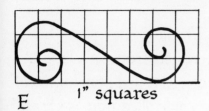

E   1" squares

Bend 18" piece of metal as in fig. E.

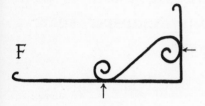

F

Arrange both bent pieces as in fig. F. Drill ⅛" holes in right-angled piece, mark through holes on to curved piece, drill curved piece for two sets of aligned holes.

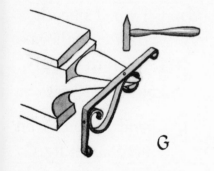

G

Rivet both pieces together, (fig. G).

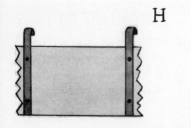

H

Drill two holes in bracket pieces, fasten to wood with screws, (fig. H).

95

Wrought-iron HOUSE MARKER

CONTINUED

I

Draw house numbers on sheet copper, brass, aluminum, or plywood, (fig. I).

Cut out numerals with jeweler's saw, (fig. J).

J

Fasten numerals to board, using escutcheon pins, (fig. K).

K

Fig. L is your sign hanging on its bracket.

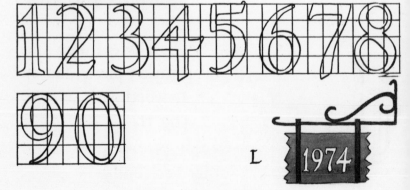

L

Wrought-iron BOOK-ENDS

MATERIALS: 4 pcs. cold rolled iron, 1/16" x 3/4" x 12"
4 pcs. cold rolled iron, 1/16" x 3/4" x 8"
1/16" drill, center punch,
1/16" iron rivets

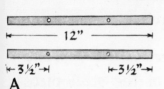

A

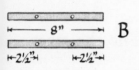

Drill 1/16" holes in all four
wrought iron pieces as in
figs. A and B.

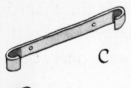

B

C

Bend ends as in fig. C.
(See p. 88).

D

Form right angle, fig. D

Rivet four pieces together
as in fig. E. Glue felt to
undersides to protect
tabletop.

E

Repeat procedure to make
other book end.

97

CHASING TOOL

MATERIALS: files, emery cloth #0, ball peen hammer, large pliers, ¼" tool steel, round or square

File a deep notch 4" from the end of the steel piece. Break it off by bending, (fig. A).

A

File one end flat. File the other end as in fig. B.
Anneal the piece: Heat the shaped end until it is a cherry red. Cool it slowly. Brighten it with emery cloth.

Hold the shaped end against an old file. Strike sharply with hammer, (fig.C). The soft end will receive the imprint of the hard file's teeth, as in fig. D.

B

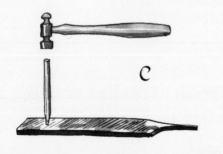

C

D

Heat about 1" of the shaped end over a gas flame until it is cherry red, then plunge vertically into cold water, fig. E.

E

The rod is now hard, but brittle. Brighten it with emery cloth. Heat the middle of the tool over a gas flame, until the shaped end is a dull straw color, (fig. F). Plunge into cold water, then polish with emery cloth.

F

Other useful shapes are shown in fig. G. These tools may also be used for wood and leather if they are made with a coarse texture.

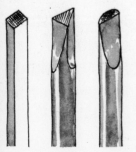

G

PAPER KNIFE

MATERIALS: sheet plastic or metal, 18 gauge, pencil and paper, rubber cement, jeweler's saw, #00 emery cloth, crocus cloth, silver polish

Use a pencil to draw the paper knife design on paper. (See designs on pp. 102, 103. These designs are suitable for both plastic and metal). (fig. A).

-A

Use rubber cement to coat both the surface of the paper and the surface of the material to which it is to be glued. Wait about five minutes, then press the paper into place, (fig. B).

B

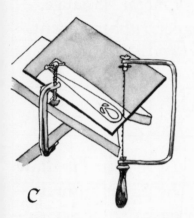

Cut out the paper knife, using a jeweler's saw. (See p. 48). Saw outside the line, using an even, vertical stroke without pressure, (fig. C).

C

Smooth all edges with #00 emery cloth or a fine file. Repeat, using crocus cloth.

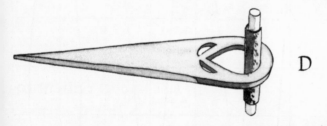

D

Inside curved edges may be reached by wrapping a bit of emery cloth around a dowel, round pencil, or other smooth, round surface, (fig. D).

(For metal polishing directions, see p. 25).

PAPER KNIFE DESIGNS

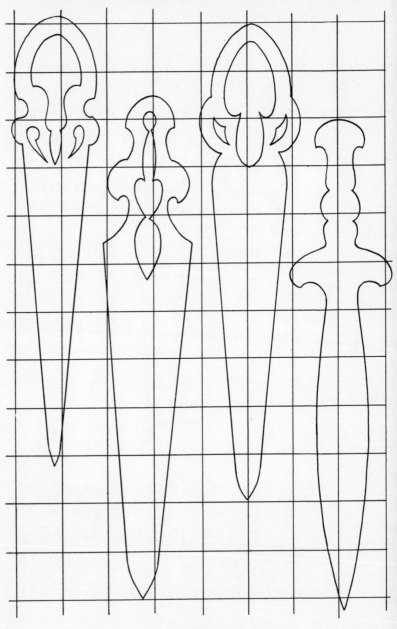

WEDGING BOARD

MATERIALS: 2 pieces of wood, 3/4" x 10" x 15"
1 piece of wood, 3/4" x 10" x 10 3/4"
2 ft. piano wire, pliers, 2 large screw eyes

(Lumber sizes are approximate. Use any standard lumber.)

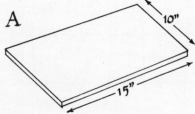

A

Cut lumber for base, (fig. A).

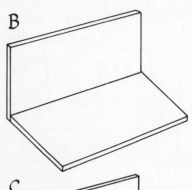

B

Cut similar piece and nail it to first piece, as in fig. B.

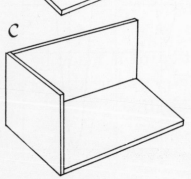

C

Cut third piece and nail it to first two, as in fig. C.

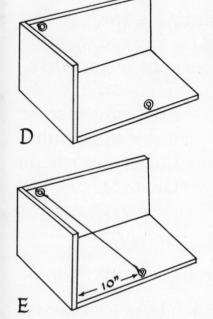

Insert two screw eyes. Top screw eye is 2" from corner. Bottom screw eye is about 10" from side, (fig. D).

Use pliers to stretch piano wire between two screw eyes. Wire must be taut, and securely fastened so that it cannot work loose.

The wedging board should be as large as possible. High back and sides prevent clay from spattering all over while wedging.

A more permanent board is made by using waterproof glue on the edges of the boards before nailing.

MAKING A PLASTER TILE

Do plaster casting on a smooth surface such as wood or glass. Exposed wood surfaces must be sized first.

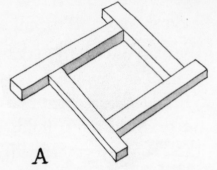

To mix size: Dissolve a little soap in some water, then brush it liberally over the surface to be sized. This prevents plaster from sticking.

A

Arrange wood as in fig. A.

Wedge clay against sides to hold wood in place. Size the wood.

Mix plaster: Sift plaster of paris into water until no more is absorbed. Stir gently for a moment, then pour into wooden form. Remove excess plaster with stick, (fig. B).

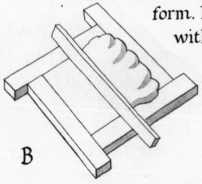

Next day, remove wooden form, leaving tile.

B

DAMP BOX FOR CLAY

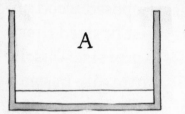

Obtain, or construct a wooden box. Pour two inches of plaster of paris into the bottom, (fig. A).

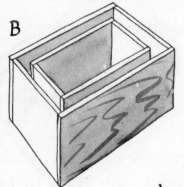

Use four boards to make a smaller box which is placed inside the first, leaving about two inches between walls. Hold these boards together with gobs of clay on the inside, no nails, (fig. B).

Size the small box only, then pour plaster of paris into the space between the two boxes. When dry, remove the inner walls, leaving a box with plaster bottom and sides.

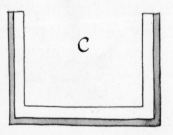

Moist clay, unfinished pieces and slip may be stored in this box provided plaster walls and bottom are wet down occasionally. The box should have a well-fitting cover.

CLAY MODELING TOOLS

Use a kitchen knife for rough cutting and shaping, fig. A.

A

B

Whittle an orange stick to make a modeling tool, (fig. B).

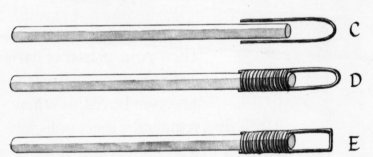
C

D

E

Shape hairpins with pliers. Bind in place with strong thread. Coat with nail polish, (figures C, D, E).

POTTERY ASH TRAY

MATERIALS: ceramic clay, wedging board, knife

Knead and wedge a handful of clay. Shape it into a ball, (fig. A).

Pound ball flat, (fig. B). This should be about ⅜" thick.

Cut a triangle from the flat clay as in fig. C.

Bend up the corners of the tri-angle as in fig. D.

Shape the finished piece so that it will hold a ciga-rette, (figs. E, F).

CLAY TILES

Knead and wedge clay to be used. This clay should be rather stiff for making tiles. Too much moisture will cause warping or cracking when drying. Add a little fine sand to the clay if this occurs.

Work on a piece of oilcloth.

Nail two parallel strips of ½" wood to the working surface. The distance between the strips is the width of the tile, (fig. A).

Dust the cloth and the wood lightly with dry, powdered clay. This will prevent clay from sticking to the form.

Use a rolling pin to roll a chunk of clay between the wood strips, forming a slab of even thickness, (fig. B).

Run a knife blade between the clay and the wooden sides. Remove the clay slab. If the clay is too

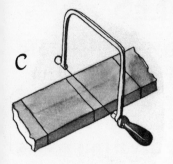

C

moist, permit it to dry a bit.

Cut the tile to size by using either a knife or a wire stretched tight in a coping saw frame, as in fig. C. Permit the tile to dry until it is almost leather hard.

D

Scrape ¼" of clay from the back of the tile, leaving margins of about ½", (fig. D).

When thoroughly dry, it may be made perfectly flat by rubbing lightly on a sheet of sand paper.

The tile is now ready for firing. If it is not to be fired, it may be decorated with tempera paints, then shellacked.

Some ceramic workers prefer to add "grog" to clay to prevent warping and cracking. Grog is made by pulverizing biscuit fired ware, (unglazed pottery), then sifting it carefully to remove large pieces.

CLAY MASK

MATERIALS: modeling clay, properly conditioned and wedged, plaster tile, clay modeling tool.

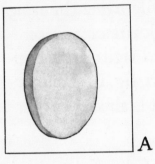

Place an egg-shaped lump of wedged clay upon a soaked plaster tile, (fig. A).

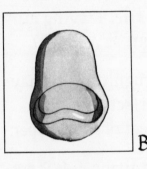

Add to bottom, making it pear-shaped, and gouge mouth with thumbs, (fig. B).

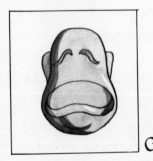

Gouge slits for eyes, add ears and chin, (fig. C).

D

Add nose and cheeks, smoothing firmly into place, (fig. D).

When piece is dry enough to handle, draw a taut wire under it, severing it from the tile. Scoop clay from the back, leaving a 1" shell, (fig. E).

Permit mask to dry slowly. Decorate it with showcard, tempera or oil colors if it is not to be fired.

E

MORE MASKS
YOU CAN MAKE

113

COIL BUILT BOWL

MATERIALS: modeling clay, properly wedged, plaster tile, kitchen knife, compass, slip

A

Prepare a batch of clay by kneading and wedging. Roll a small quantity into a ball, (fig. A).

B

Beat the ball into a flat slab about ¼" thick. This is done on a plaster tile. (See p. 106). (fig. B).

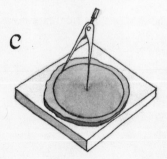

C

Scribe a circle. This forms the base of the bowl, (fig. C).

D

Trim away all excess clay from the base, (fig. D).

E

Scratch up the surface about ½" inside the circular base, (fig. E).

F

Use the palms of your hands to form a long, even roll about ½" thick, or slightly thicker than the walls of the piece you are making. Moisten the scratched surface of the base with slip. Coil the clay rope on the base, so that there is a slight overlap at the edges, (fig. F). Use your fingers to unite the coil with the base.

115

COIL BUILT BOWL
CONTINUED

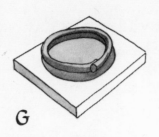

G

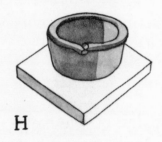

H

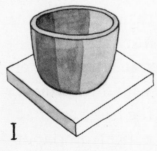

I

Scratch the surface of the coil you have just laid. Moisten it with slip. Now lay another coil atop the first one, so that the ends do not coincide with the ends of the coil beneath, (fig. G). Use your fingers to unite the second coil with the first.

Continue to add coils, first scratching the surface, then adding slip to the coil upon which you are building,(fig. H). Fig. I represents the finished bowl.

While building the sides, smooth them with your fingers, but do not pinch the walls, as this would tend to widen the piece at that point. Do not permit incomplete pieces to dry out. They must be kept in a clay bin, or covered with a wet cloth.

POTTERY TEMPLATES

Pottery pieces with graceful curves may be built by the coil method, provided a guide is used in forming the walls. Such a guide is called a template, and it may be made of cardboard, plywood, ½" wood, sheet zinc, or galvanized iron.

The cardboard template is merely used as a guide to which the walls of the piece are brought as they are built coil by coil. Wood and metal templates serve the same purpose, but they may be scraped around the sides of the piece as it is being built to "true" it to exact, symmetrical shape. Too much clay should not be removed with the template, otherwise the walls will become too thin. Too much pressure applied with the template will stretch and distort the shape of the piece. It is best to build the walls right up to the template curve, scraping away as little as possible. Large pieces should not be built at one sitting, as the walls may collapse when they are soft. In that case, build your piece several inches at a time, allowing the piece to dry nearly "leather hard" between work periods.

POTTERY TEMPLATES

TO MAKE A TEMPLATE:
On paper, draw the outside
curve of the proposed pottery piece, (fig. A).

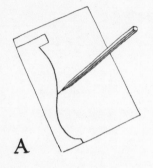

Trace this curve on to your
template material (wood or
metal), as in fig. B.

A

Cut out the template, leaving
a straight bottom edge,
and sufficient width to
enable you to hold it
easily, (fig. C). Cut metal
templates with tin snips,
then file edges and
smooth them with emery
cloth. Make wooden templates
of ½″ wood or ¼″ plywood. Cut
curves with coping saw, file
and sand all edges smooth,
then finish with two coats of
of shellac.

B

C

POTTERY TEMPLATE PATTERNS

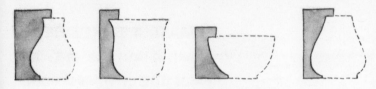

TEMPLATE PATTERNS
(USE ½" SQUARES)

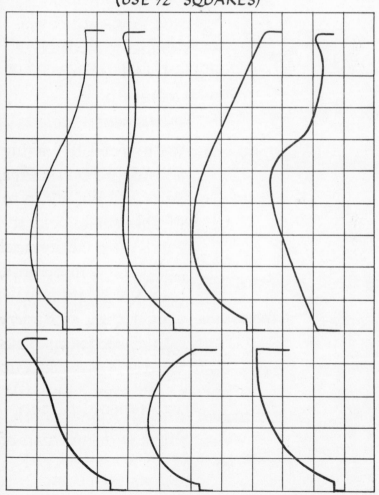

LEATHER TOOLS

MALLET: for striking leather tools. Do not use a hammer, since it mars the tool ends.

DRIVE PUNCH: struck with a mallet to produce holes for lacing.

SPACING WHEEL: rolled against a straight edge, leaving evenly spaced marks for punching lacing holes.

SPRING PUNCH (single): used for punching lacing holes. No. #0 is used for 3/32" lacing.

ROTARY PUNCH: six tube punch with sizes used for lacing, setting snap buttons, eyelets, etc.

THONGING CHISEL: for making slits for lacing, instead of holes.

TRACER: for tracing designs on leather. (See p. 128).

EXTENSION KNIFE: As the blade wears, it can be renewed by pulling out from handle.

FID: for enlarging holes, tightening lacing, stippling.

EDGE CREASER: pressed down and drawn along the edge of a piece to produce a finished edge.

MODELING TOOL: the most commonly used shape for line tooling, flat modeling and repoussé. Other shapes are available.

121

LEATHER TOOLS
CONTINUED

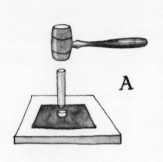

EYELET SETTER: A hole is punched in the leather, the eyelet is pushed through, the leather and eyelet are placed on a maple board. The tool is held vertically, centered in the eyelet, then struck with a mallet to spread the eye, (fig. A).

A

"C" CLAMP: useful for holding belts, lanyards for braiding.

STIPPLER: is pressed against the surface of the leather to produce a stipple.

SNAP BUTTON OUTFIT: for setting both large and small snap buttons in leather projects. See opposite page for instructions.

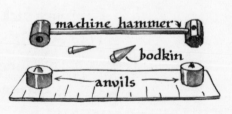

machine hammer

bodkin

anvils

HOW TO SET SNAP BUTTONS

 cap

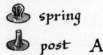 eyelet

spring

post   A

A snap button consists of four parts: a cap and eyelet, which go together in the flap or upper piece of leather, and a spring and post which go together in the lower piece, (fig. A).

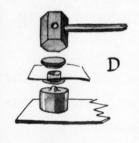

C

Make a hole for the eyelet with #7 punch. Place bodkin into eyelet, and push from back of leather, through hole, as in figs. B and C.

D

Place eyelet on large anvil of snap button outfit. Place cap over eyelet, and end of machine hammer over the cap. Strike sharply with hammer to set, (fig D).

E

Make a hole for the post with a #1 punch. Push post through back of leather, place spring over it and the small end of the machine hammer over the spring. Strike with a hammer to set, (fig. E).

123

LEATHER STAMPING TOOL

MATERIALS: 3/8" dowel stick, coping saw, triangular file, sand paper

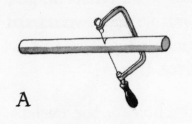

A

Cut the dowel into 4" lengths, (fig. A).

File the dowel so that the top is perfectly flat and smooth, (fig. B). Then, sandpaper the top very lightly to remove the sharp edge.

B

File a shallow notch across the top of the dowel, dividing the area in half, as in fig. C.

File another notch, as in fig. D, dividing the top into even quarters.

The tool is now ready for use. After preparing the leather for tooling, place the notched end against the leather and strike it a light blow with a mallet.

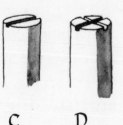

C   D

PATTERN IDEAS, USING STAMPING DOWELS

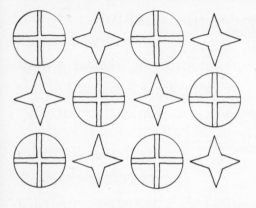

Alternate design, using two stamps.

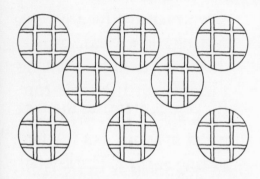

Drop repeat de-sign, using one stamp.

These patterns can be made by using woodcarving tools on the dowel ends.

Areas to be cut out are shaded.

CUTTING LEATHER

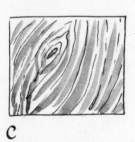

A

B

Use a sharp knife. Fig. A shows an extension knife. Fig. B shows a mat-cutting knife. Both are suitable for leather cutting.

Cut on a smooth, soft, clear-grained board. A drawing board is recommended for leather cutting. Soft, clear, pine should be used for making a leather cutting table top. Fig. C shows the type of wood to avoid as a leather cutting surface. The knots and coarse grain may turn the knife point, causing inaccuracies.

C

D

Use a steel square for cutting straight pieces, (fig. D).

Press the knife firmly against the edge of the square. Cut firmly, going through the leather in one stroke at a 45 degree angle, (fig. E). Heavy scissors or tin snips may be used for cutting curves.

E

A template is a guide used either in marking out a piece of work or in cutting a particular shape. Templates may be cut from galvanized sheet iron, using a pair of tin snips. File and smooth all edges with emery cloth. The use of a template eliminates waste, (fig. F).

F

Use templates when cutting pieces from a skin. That part of the skin which formed the back of the animal contains the best leather, and should be used for billfolds, wallets, and other projects requiring firm stock. The edges of the skin may be used for small pieces.

LEATHER TOOLING-*LineDesign*

MATERIALS: modeling tool, tracing tool or hard pencil, sponge, water, plate glass, marble, hardwood or galvanized iron sheet

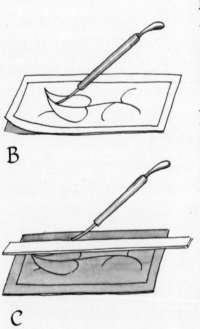

Moisten the back of the leather with a sponge, until it assumes an even, dark tone, (fig. A).

A

Place the leather, face up, on a sheet of plate glass, marble, hardwood, or galvanized iron.

Place paper with design over the leather. Trace with hard pencil or tracing tool, (fig. B).

B

Go over design with modeling tool. Use ruler for straight lines, (fig. C).

C

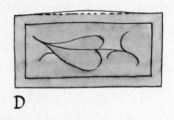

If the leather puckers while it is being worked, it is too dry; moisten it slightly. If water oozes when working, it is too wet. Permit it to dry a bit.

D

Use a sharp knife to trim the piece to exact size, since leather sometimes stretches after tooling. The dotted line shows a piece that might be cut away, (fig. D).

If the piece is to be used as part of a project and must be laced, the holes are now marked and punched. (See pp. 41, 134-8).

PRACTICE DESIGNS FOR LINE TOOLING

LEATHER TOOLING-*Flat Modeling*

Prepare the leather, and tool the design, following the steps described on p.128. You now have a line design.

A

Using the broad end of a modeling tool, depress the background areas, leaving the design raised. In the case of a monogram the letter would appear raised as the background is pressed down, (fig.A). The areas to be depressed are indicated by a dark tone.

Backgrounds may also be textured by stippling with the pointed end of a modeling tool, or by stamping with a background texturing tool. (See p. 125).

LEATHER TOOLING-*Repoussé Modeling*

In repoussé modeling, the design is pushed from the back so that it is raised from the flat surface of the background.

First, tool the outline of the design.

Place the leather, face down, on the palm of one hand. With the broad end of the modeling tool, press down that part of the design that is to be raised. Face up, depress the background around the raised design. Let it dry flat.

DESIGNS FOR FLAT MODELING AND REPOUSSÉ

131

TOOLED BOOKMARK DESIGNS

*Designs are first tooled in line,
then, if so desired, flat modeled*

Cut on lines indicated to make a fringed end

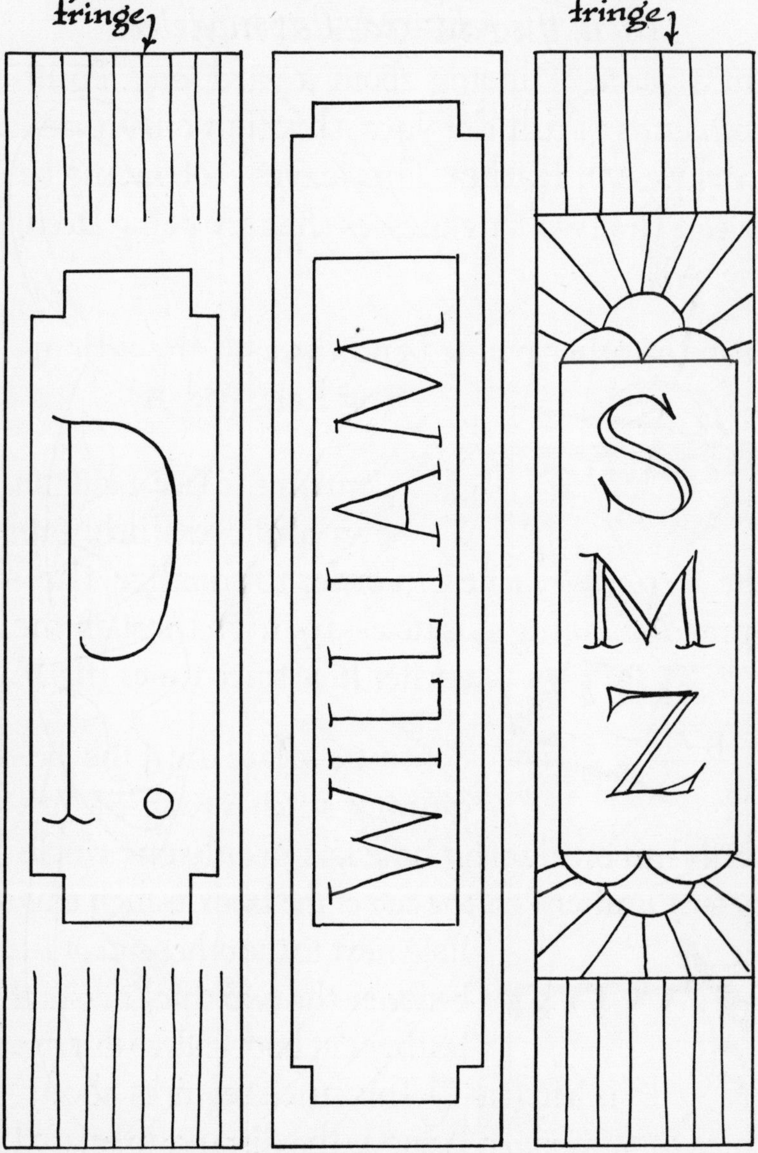

fringe↓   fringe↓

D.

WILLIAM

S
M
Z

LEATHER LACING STITCHES
(See p. 41 for Leather Lacing Instructions)

OVER AND OVER STITCH

Cut a piece of lacing about a yard long. Point both ends. Push 1" of lace through only one thickness of leather. This leaves 1" of lacing between the two thicknesses that are being laced, (fig. A).

Push the other pointed end through the adjoining hole, (fig. A).

Continue to lace, using an over and over stitch, until the corner is reached. In order to equalize the spread of lacing it is necessary to go through the corner hole three times, (fig. B).

Continue to lace until the beginning stitch is reached. You will find one lacing hole left, in only one thickness of leather. Pass the end of the lace through this hole, next to the other end of lace, between the two thicknesses of leather. Cut both ends so that about ½" is left, (fig. C). This stitch requires about three times as much lacing as the distance to be laced.

IN AND OUT STITCH

This stitch is frequently used for decoration on a single thickness of leather. It may be used for holding celluloid windows in place, as in picture frames and wallets.

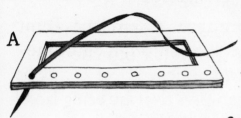

Punch an even number of holes for this stitch. Beginning with the first hole at either end, push the pointed end of the lace through, for about an inch, (fig. A).

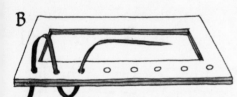

Push the other pointed lace end down through the next hole, and up through the following one, (fig. B).

Continue to lace until the end of the piece is reached. Cut off the ends, so that about ½" is left, and cement them firmly to the bottom of the leather, (fig. C). This stitch requires about one and one-half times as much lacing as the distance to be laced.

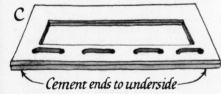

Cement ends to underside

135

LEATHER LACING STITCHES

CONTINUED

LOOP, OR BUTTONHOLE STITCH

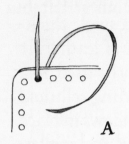

Pass 1" of pointed lacing through a punched hole, (fig. A).

A

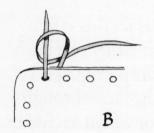

Hold the short end vertically. Loop other end as in fig.B.

B

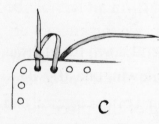

Tighten lace around the short end, as in fig. C. Bring the long end of lace around the front, and through the next hole.

C

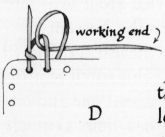

working end

Next, bring the working end of the lace around the front, and through the loop left by the previous stitch, (fig. D).

D

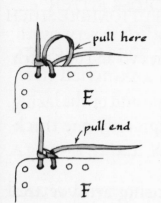

pull here

E

Tighten previous stitch, but leave the loop, as in fig. E.

pull end

F

Pull the end of the lace to finish the stitch, (fig. F).

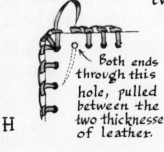

G

Continue to lace, as in fig. G.

TO FINISH LACING: Remove the first vertical end, (fig. A), from its loop. Pull it through its hole, between the two thicknesses of leather. Bring other end down through the loop formerly occupied by the vertical end, and through the same hole. Both ends are now between the two leather pieces. Pull tight, and cut off, leaving about ½", (fig. H).

Both ends through this hole, pulled between the two thicknesses of leather.

H

This stitch requires five times as much lacing as the distance to be laced.

LEATHER LACING STITCHES

CROSS STITCH

This stitch is very much like the over and over stitch.

Pass one end of the lacing through only one thickness of leather, as in fig. A.

A

Lace, using an over and over stitch, going through every other hole, (fig. B).

B

When completely laced, double back and lace the holes that have been left out, working in the opposite direction, (fig. C).

C

End the lacing as for the over and over stitch.
(See p. 134).

This stitch requires twice as much lacing as the over and over stitch.

SPLICING LACING

It is frequently necessary to splice lacing that has broken, or to add a piece in order to finish a job. The procedure is simple:

The end is tapered, with a flat, slicing cut on the unfinished side of the lace, (fig. A).

A

Taper one end of the lace to be added, as in fig. B. This cut is made on the finished side of the lace.

B

Coat each of the cut ends with rubber cement. When dry, press them together. Finished splice as in fig C.

C

Point lace for working by cutting at an angle as in fig. D.

D

Some workers prefer to stiffen the end of the lace by coating it with household cement, then allowing it to dry. This makes lacing easier.

ONE-PIECE BILLFOLD

MATERIALS: tooling leather, edge creaser, cutting knife, snap button set, snap button

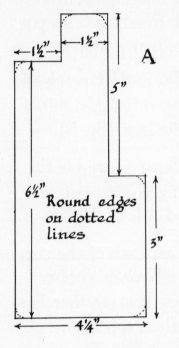

A

Cut a template, using dimensions as given in fig. A. (See p.126 for cutting directions).

Mark the piece on leather, then cut it out. Round all corners, as shown by dotted lines in fig. A. Leather from the back of the animal's hide should be used for this project, since it will encounter hard wear.

Moisten the piece as for tooling, then place it face up, on a tooling surface, (maple board, glass or sheet tin).

B

Use the edge creaser to depress a line all around the piece, (fig. B).

With the piece still moist, fold down the flap, as in fig. C. Next, fold up the long flap, as in fig. D. Now fold the piece in half, from left to right,

C   D

leaving only the short flap showing, (fig. E).

E   F

Place the folded article under a weight until it is dry. Then, unfold the billfold, and mark and insert a snap button. (See p.123 for instructions). Fig. F shows finished billfold.

Smooth leathers may be tooled before folding. Leathers with grained surfaces should be left in natural state.

COIN PURSE

MATERIALS: tooling leather, modeling tool, cutting knife, #0 punch, spacing wheel, goatskin lace 3/32", rubber cement, snap button, snap button set

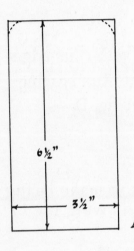

Cut leather as shown in fig. A. Round corners (dotted lines).

A

Use pencil to mark piece as in fig. B. Tooling is applied to space indicated. See p. 128.

B

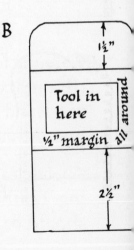

1½"

Tool in here

½" margin all around

2½"

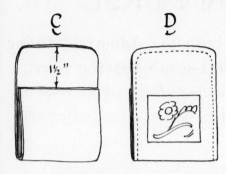

Bend piece as shown in fig. C. Glue edges down with rubber cement. Run spacing wheel 3/8" from edge as in fig. D.

Use #0 punch to make lacing holes, (fig. E).

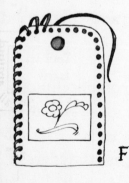

Lace piece, (fig. F). See p. 134. See p. 123 for snap button directions.

143

POCKET PHOTO FRAME

MATERIALS: leather, cutting knife and board, steel angle, #0 punch, 3/32" goatskin lace, rubber cement, celluloid

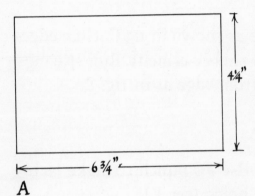

Cut a piece of leather 6¾" x 4¼", as in fig. A. This is for the back.

A

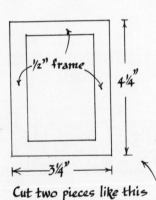

½" frame

4¼"

3¼"

Cut two pieces like this

B

Cut <u>two</u> pieces of leather 3¼" x 4¼". These are for the two windows. Cut out the center pieces, leaving a half-inch frame all around, (fig. B).

Cut two pieces of celluloid, exactly the same size as the frames (3¼" x 4¼"). Use rubber cement to glue the edges of the celluloid to the frames, (fig. C

Punch lacing holes ⅛″ from the inside edge. Use the IN-AND-OUT STITCH as in fig. D, lacing the celluloid to the frame.

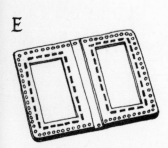

Glue the frames to the back, place under a weight until dry. Round the corners slightly, and punch holes for lacing 3/16″ from the outside edge. Use a spacing wheel to mark the places where holes are to be punched, (fig. E).

Lace the outside of the frame.(For lacing directions, see p.p. 134-8).

Fold the completed frame in half, and place it under a weight for a day. Pictures may be inserted from the center of the frame under the celluloid windows.

Fig. F shows completed frame.

145

WALLET BILLFOLD

MATERIALS: tooling leather, cutting knife and board, celluloid, household cement, 3/32" lace, #0 punch, spacing wheel

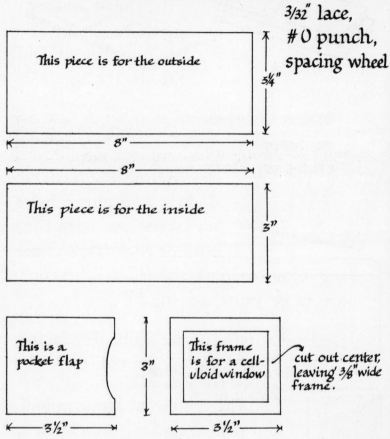

This piece is for the outside

3¼"

8"

8"

This piece is for the inside

3"

This is a pocket flap

3"

3½"

This frame is for a celluloid window

cut out center, leaving ⅜" wide frame.

3½"

Cut leather pieces to dimensions shown on this page.

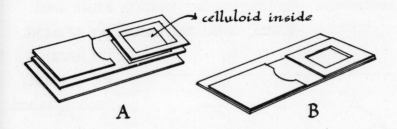

celluloid inside

A   B

Wallet is assembled as in fig. A. Use rubber cement to glue edges of pieces together, then press under weight, (fig. B).

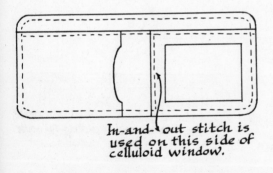

In-and-out stitch is used on this side of celluloid window.

Cut corners round. Run spacing wheel all around, ⅜" from edge. Use #0 punch, and lace. See p. 134 for lacing directions.

DOUBLE MONOGRAMS

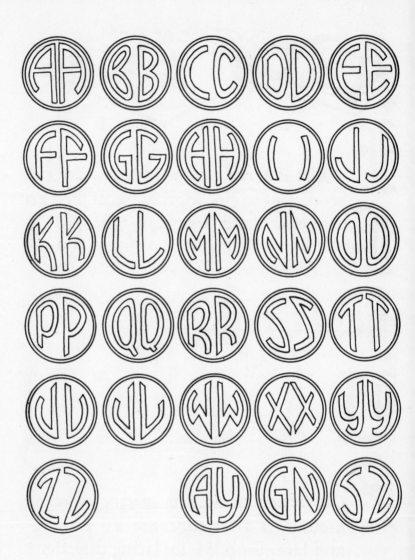

OLD ENGLISH INITIALS

ABCDE
FGHIJ
KLMNO
PQRST
UVWXY
Z

TRIPLE MONOGRAMS

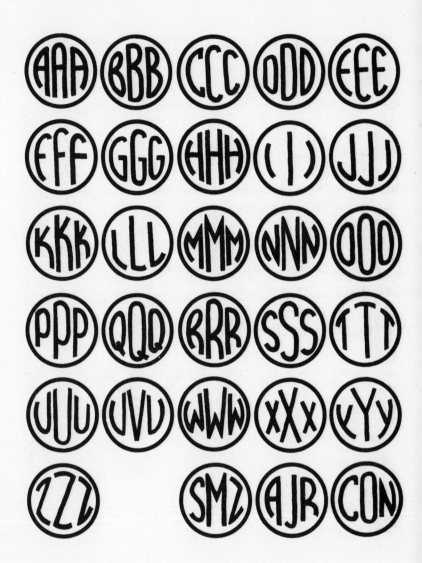

SCRIPT INITIALS

A B C D E
F G H I J
K L M N O
P Q R S T
U V W X Y
Z

INDEX